Detecting
the Past

CONTENTS

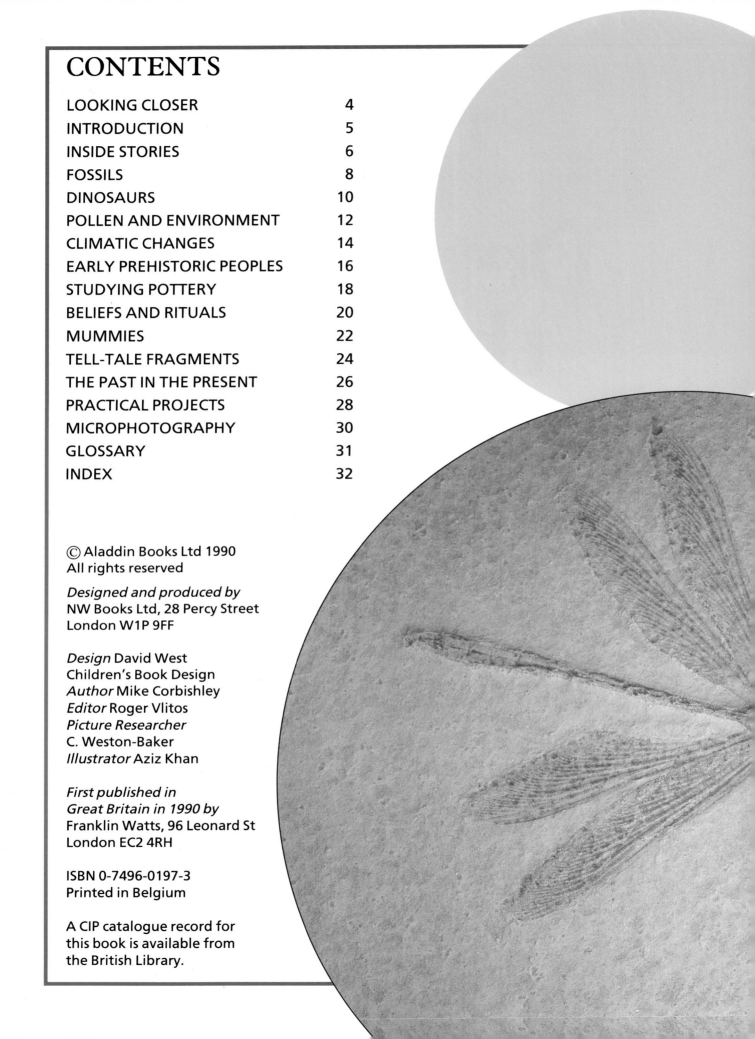

Designed and produced by
NW Books Ltd, 28 Percy Street
London W1P 9FF

Design David West
Children's Book Design
Author Mike Corbishley
Editor Roger Vlitos
Picture Researcher
C. Weston-Baker
Illustrator Aziz Khan

*First published in
Great Britain in 1990 by*
Franklin Watts, 96 Leonard St
London EC2 4RH

ISBN 0-7496-0197-3
Printed in Belgium

A CIP catalogue record for
this book is available from
the British Library.

THROUGH · THE · MICROSCOPE
Detecting the Past

Mike Corbishley

FRANKLIN WATTS
London: New York: Toronto: Sydney

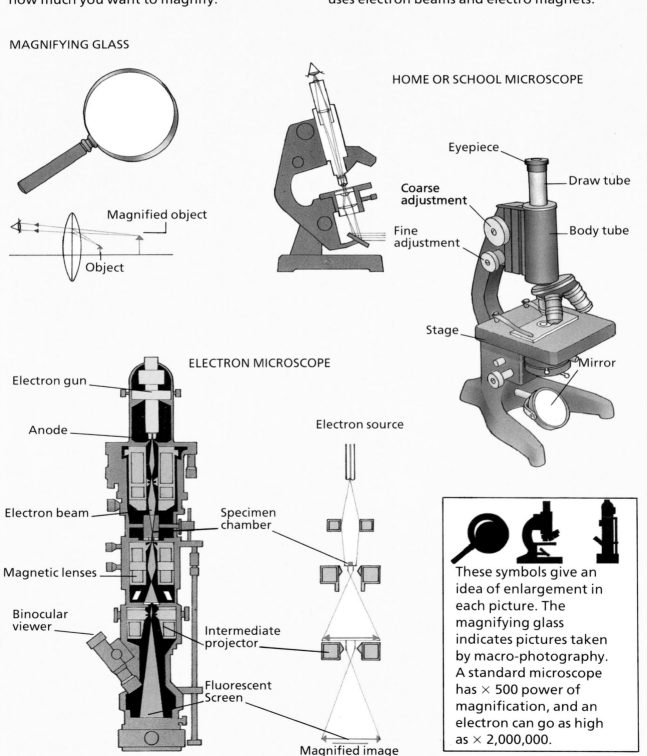

LOOKING CLOSER

Microscopes and magnifying glasses work by using lenses and light. A lens is usually a thin, circular glass, thicker in the middle, which bends rays of light so that when you look through it an object appears enlarged. A microscope uses several lenses. It will also have a set of adjustments to give you a choice over how much you want to magnify.

When we want to view something under a microscope it must be small enough to fit on a glass slide. This is put on the stage over the mirror and light is reflected through so that the lenses inside can magnify the view for us. But not all microscopes work this way. The greatest detail can be seen with an electron microscope which uses electron beams and electro magnets.

MAGNIFYING GLASS

Magnified object

Object

HOME OR SCHOOL MICROSCOPE

Eyepiece

Draw tube

Coarse adjustment

Fine adjustment

Body tube

Stage

Mirror

ELECTRON MICROSCOPE

Electron gun

Anode

Electron beam

Magnetic lenses

Binocular viewer

Specimen chamber

Intermediate projector

Fluorescent Screen

Electron source

Magnified image

These symbols give an idea of enlargement in each picture. The magnifying glass indicates pictures taken by macro-photography. A standard microscope has × 500 power of magnification, and an electron can go as high as × 2,000,000.

INTRODUCTION

5

A microscope is used to study things too small to be seen with the naked eye. This book has pictures taken through microscopes, or with special magnifying lenses attached to cameras. Drawings appear alongside to help explain what the microscopes are showing us. Geologists, palaeontologists, and archaeologists discover and write about what went on in the past. Geologists are interested in rocks and fossils. Archaeologists study the remains of people, what they were like and how they used to live. Palaeontologists do most of their work with fossils. Together they help us to understand what went on thousands of millions of years ago.

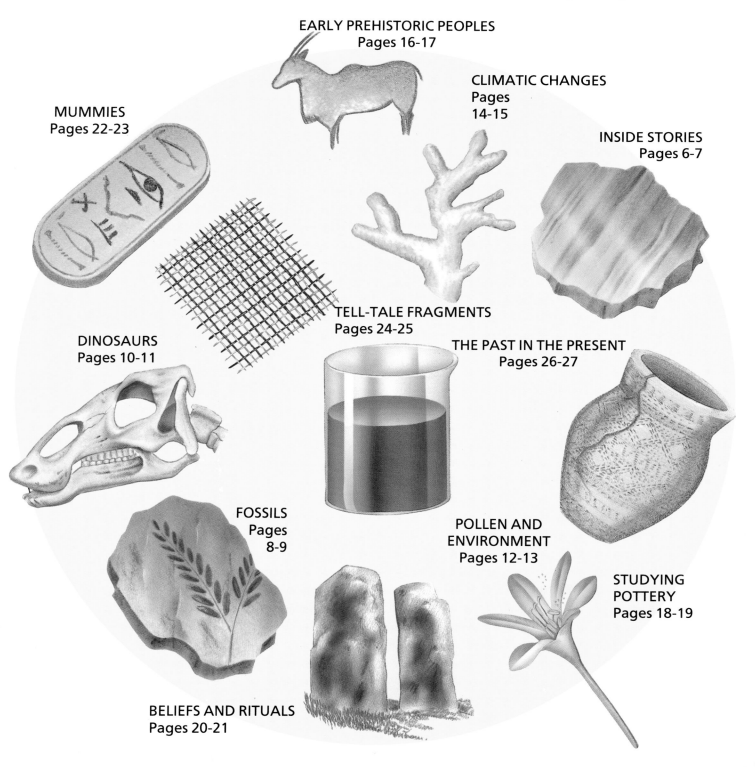

EARLY PREHISTORIC PEOPLES
Pages 16-17

CLIMATIC CHANGES
Pages 14-15

INSIDE STORIES
Pages 6-7

MUMMIES
Pages 22-23

TELL-TALE FRAGMENTS
Pages 24-25

DINOSAURS
Pages 10-11

THE PAST IN THE PRESENT
Pages 26-27

FOSSILS
Pages 8-9

POLLEN AND ENVIRONMENT
Pages 12-13

STUDYING POTTERY
Pages 18-19

BELIEFS AND RITUALS
Pages 20-21

INSIDE STORIES

Four and a half thousand million years ago the Earth was a molten mass. Gradually its surface cooled and formed a crust. This crust is still on the move as layers of rock push against each other or drift apart. Different kinds of rock have been formed on the crust which we can study today. Some were once molten material squeezed up from beneath the crust; others have been built up from layers of sand and mud (see illustration – left) others have undergone enormous change. They are called igneous, sedimentary or metamorphic rocks. However, geologists can tell us more than just how our planet was made. They use their understanding to detect the mineral resources and fuel deposits essential to our way of life today.

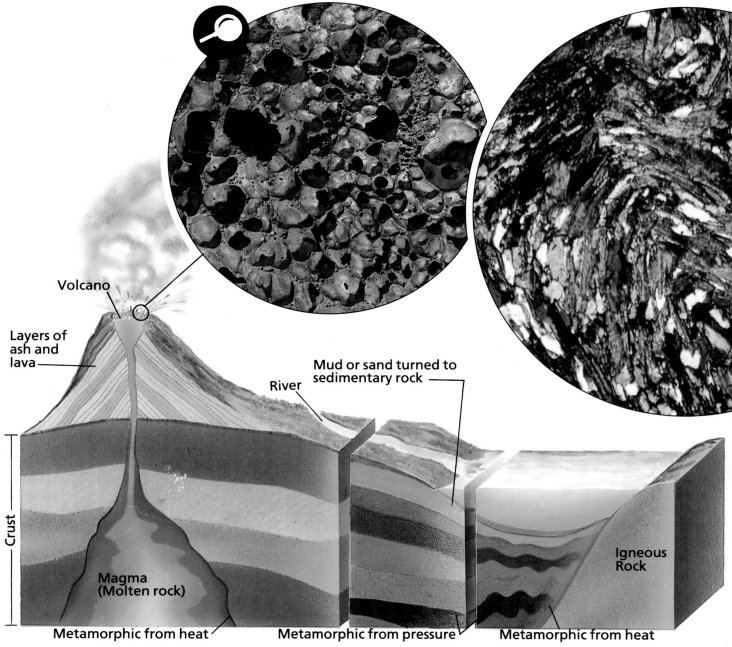

Volcano

Layers of ash and lava

River

Mud or sand turned to sedimentary rock

Crust

Magma (Molten rock)

Metamorphic from heat

Metamorphic from pressure

Metamorphic from heat

Igneous Rock

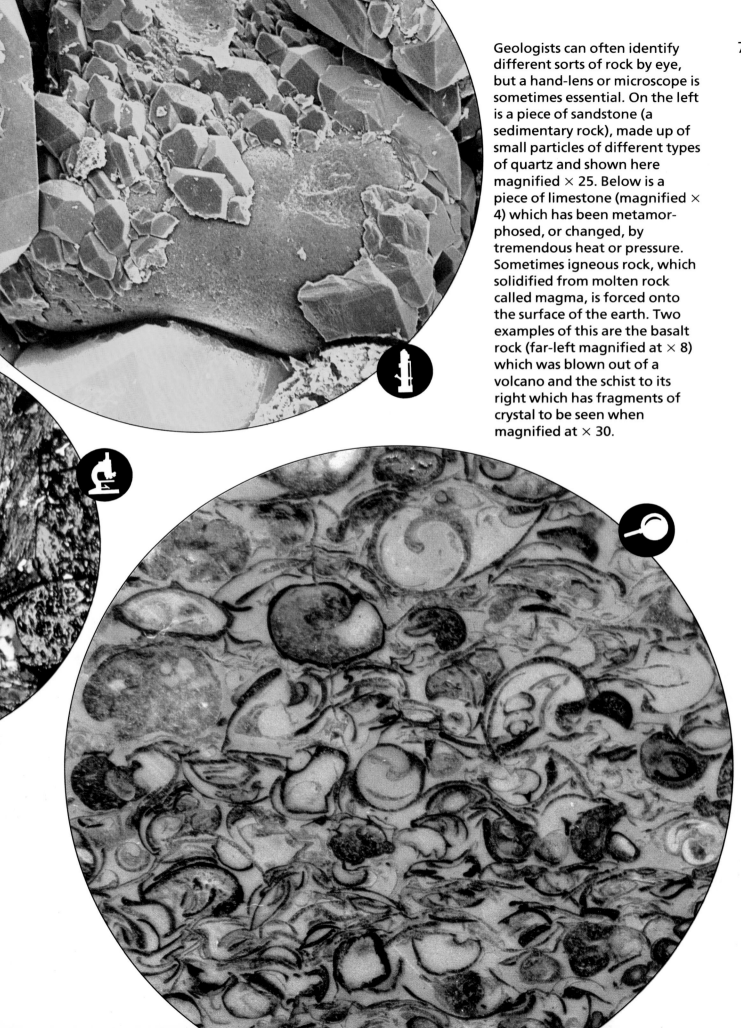

Geologists can often identify different sorts of rock by eye, but a hand-lens or microscope is sometimes essential. On the left is a piece of sandstone (a sedimentary rock), made up of small particles of different types of quartz and shown here magnified × 25. Below is a piece of limestone (magnified × 4) which has been metamorphosed, or changed, by tremendous heat or pressure. Sometimes igneous rock, which solidified from molten rock called magma, is forced onto the surface of the earth. Two examples of this are the basalt rock (far-left magnified at × 8) which was blown out of a volcano and the schist to its right which has fragments of crystal to be seen when magnified at × 30.

FOSSILS

Fossil is the word we use for the remains of animals or plants which have been preserved in or on the ground. Fossils are usually made of stone, but sometimes a whole insect is trapped, like the moth in amber on the bottom right. Often the creature or plant is replaced by stone leaving a "petrified" object. Sometimes the hardest parts survive, such as the bones of an animal. Another type, illustrated on the left, shows the print of a leaf, surviving only as a film of carbon. "Trace" fossils can be anything left behind from a dinosaur's footprint to a worm hole in what was once mud. Some rocks are made up of fossils. Coal, for instance, is mainly composed of compressed plants that lived 300 million years ago.

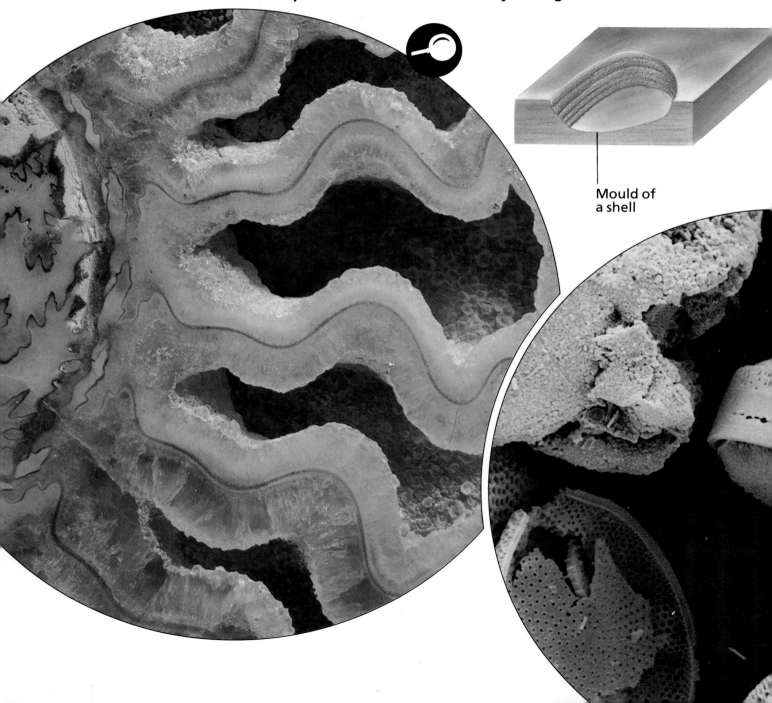

Mould of
a shell

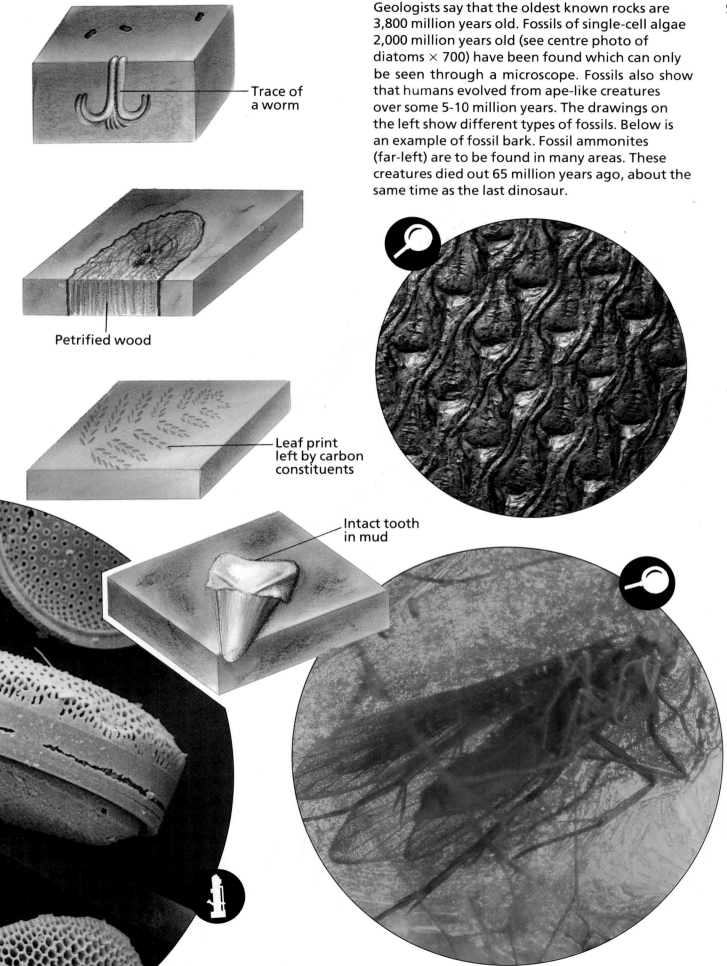

Trace of a worm

Petrified wood

Leaf print left by carbon constituents

Intact tooth in mud

Geologists say that the oldest known rocks are 3,800 million years old. Fossils of single-cell algae 2,000 million years old (see centre photo of diatoms × 700) have been found which can only be seen through a microscope. Fossils also show that humans evolved from ape-like creatures over some 5-10 million years. The drawings on the left show different types of fossils. Below is an example of fossil bark. Fossil ammonites (far-left) are to be found in many areas. These creatures died out 65 million years ago, about the same time as the last dinosaur.

DINOSAURS

Dinosaurs, the word means "terrible lizards", were reptiles which became extinct about 65 million years ago. They lived on the earth for over 140 million years but the last ones suddenly died out. This was possibly due to a rapid cooling of the planet's climate. Before that time most of the earth was warm and damp so that even in the Arctic Circle there were tropical plants and dinosaurs that ate them. Dinosaurs vanished from the earth millions of years before people evolved. We have to reconstruct what they might have looked like from their fossils. Today the animals that are related most closely to them are crocodiles and birds. Up to now scientists have discovered many hundreds of kinds of dinosaur.

The Protoceratops, when fully grown to 1.8 metres in length, had horns. The discovery of complete nests of fossil eggs (below) told scientists how dinosaurs looked after their young. The baby Protoceratops was about 30 centimetres long. The size of dinosaurs varied a lot. The Brachiosaurus, for example, was 23 metres long and weighed 80 tonnes. The Cynognathus, from which the tooth (below right) came, was only 1.5 metres long. This reptile lived 200 million years ago.

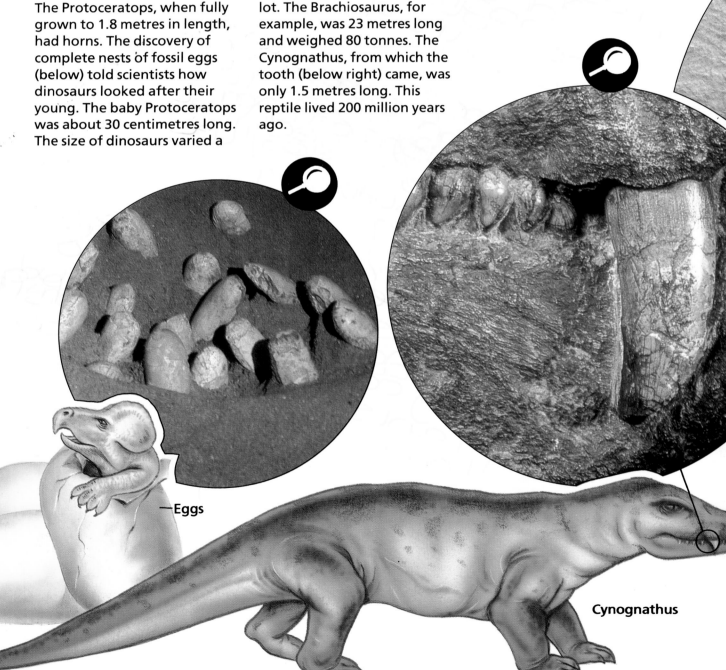

Eggs

Cynognathus

Not all creatures that lived during the "Age of the Dinosaurs" were dinosaurs. Dinosaurs lived on the land. In the air were flying reptiles called pterosaurs and in the sea were various types of swimming reptiles including plesiosaurs and ichthyosaurs.

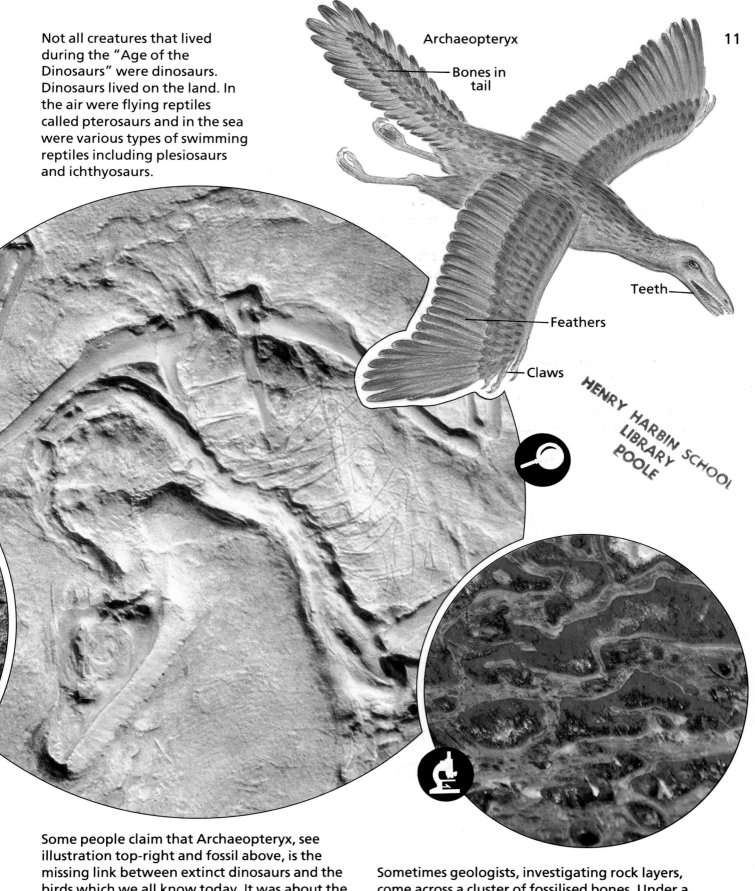

Archaeopteryx

Bones in tail

Teeth

Feathers

Claws

Some people claim that Archaeopteryx, see illustration top-right and fossil above, is the missing link between extinct dinosaurs and the birds which we all know today. It was about the same size as a modern crow and ate insects and small reptiles. These strange flying animals had feathers, jaws with sharp teeth, wing claws for climbing trees, and a long bony tail.

Sometimes geologists, investigating rock layers, come across a cluster of fossilised bones. Under a microscope (see above) these can appear to be very beautiful. Palaeontologists, scientists who specialise in fossils, will often have to study these finds in detail.

POLLEN AND ENVIRONMENT

Pollen is found in the anthers of any plants or trees which flower. It is like powder and the individual grains can only be seen through a microscope. Each pollen grain is a single cell with two coatings. The inner one, called the intine, is thin, but the outer one, the exine, is thicker and very resistant to decay or damage. This helps preserve the pollen for a long period of time. During the flowering season millions of pollen grains are constantly in the air. Many of these are trapped in places where they can be preserved, such as peat bogs. Samples can be collected by archaeologists during an excavation and studied. Pollen grains can be identified and so the types of plants and trees the pollen came from can be worked out.

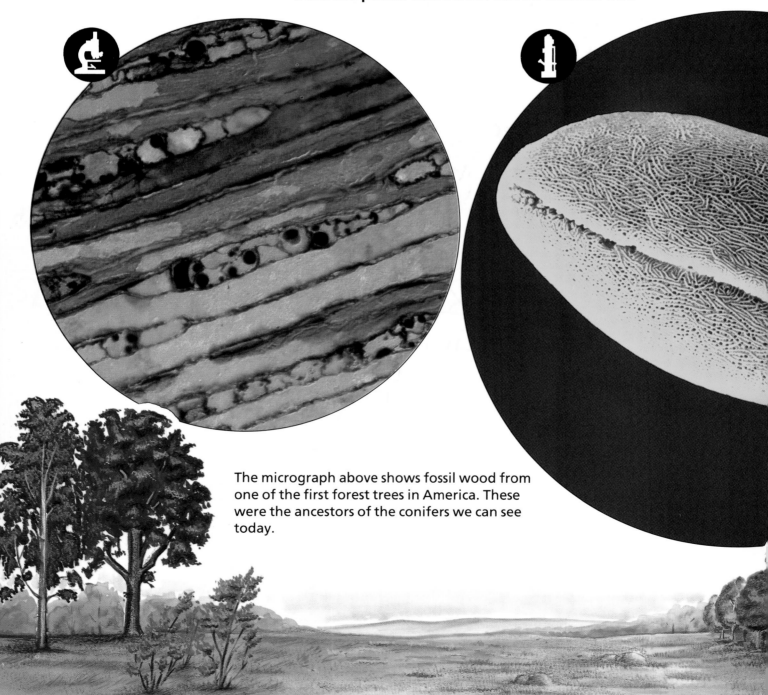

The micrograph above shows fossil wood from one of the first forest trees in America. These were the ancestors of the conifers we can see today.

Pollen grains travel only a short distance from the plants or trees they come from. We can therefore build up a good picture of a vanished environment by studying surviving pollen samples. Many kinds of prehistoric pollen grains resemble those of plants and trees alive today.

Each type of pollen grain can be recognised. The outer coatings of the two shown at the bottom of this page are different (Speedwell on the left magnified × 560, Cat's-Ear right × 486). In the middle is the pollen grain of a Hollyhock at × 665.

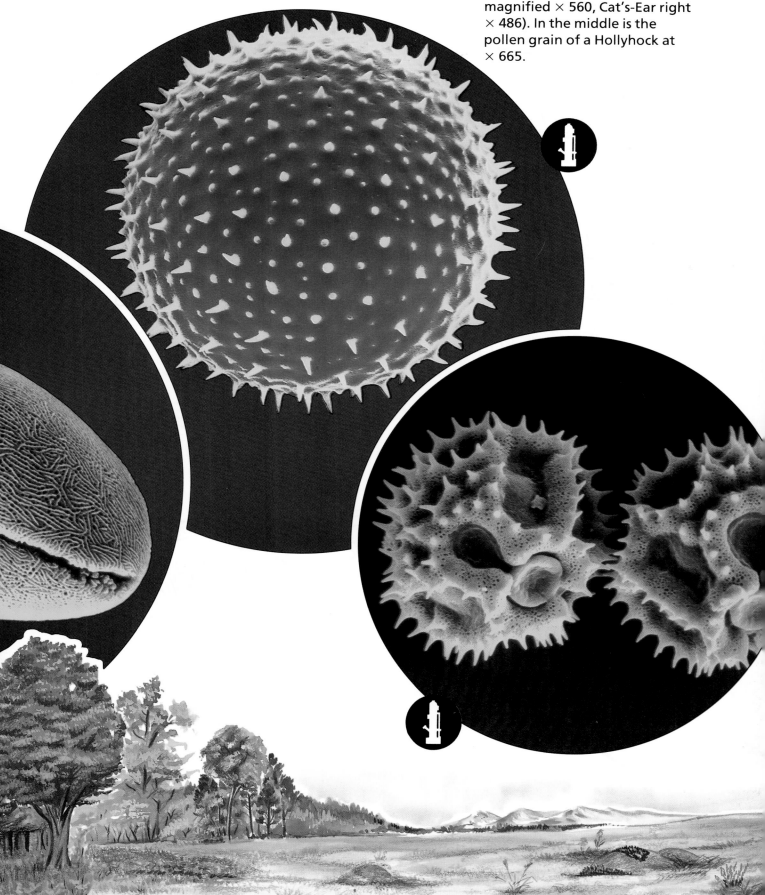

CLIMATIC CHANGES

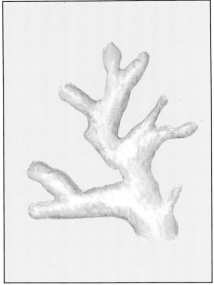

Over the past thousands of millions of years the size and the shape of the land masses and the oceans have changed enormously. The climates, or long-term patterns of weather, are also very different. In the glacial periods, or "Ice Ages", whole areas became impossible, or difficult to live in due to the cold. A good example of the way that climate can affect continents is the island of Britain. Three hundred thousand years ago Britain was joined to the continent of Europe by land. At this time the first people moved north into Britain to hunt, fish and gather their food. Between 8,000 and 7,000 years ago the climate changed and it became warmer. The ice melted, the seas rose and Britain became an island.

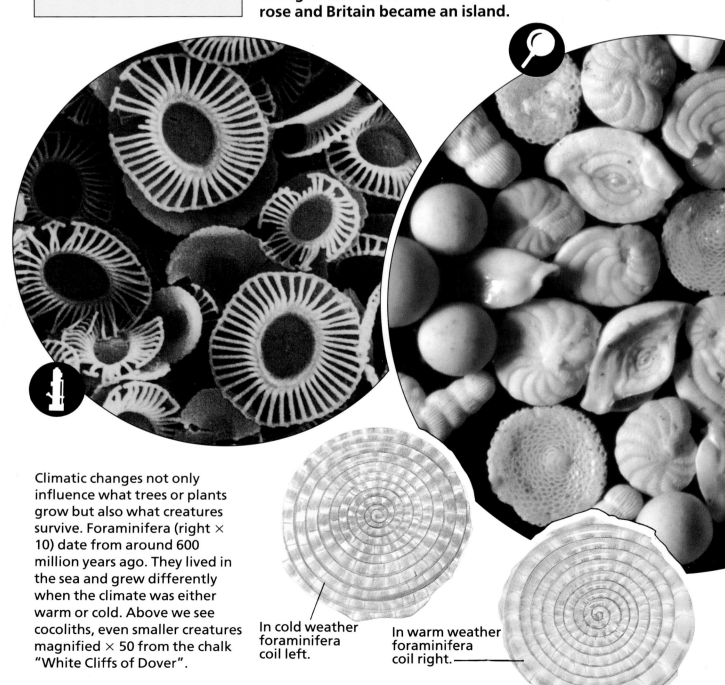

Climatic changes not only influence what trees or plants grow but also what creatures survive. Foraminifera (right × 10) date from around 600 million years ago. They lived in the sea and grew differently when the climate was either warm or cold. Above we see cocoliths, even smaller creatures magnified × 50 from the chalk "White Cliffs of Dover".

In cold weather foraminifera coil left.

In warm weather foraminifera coil right.

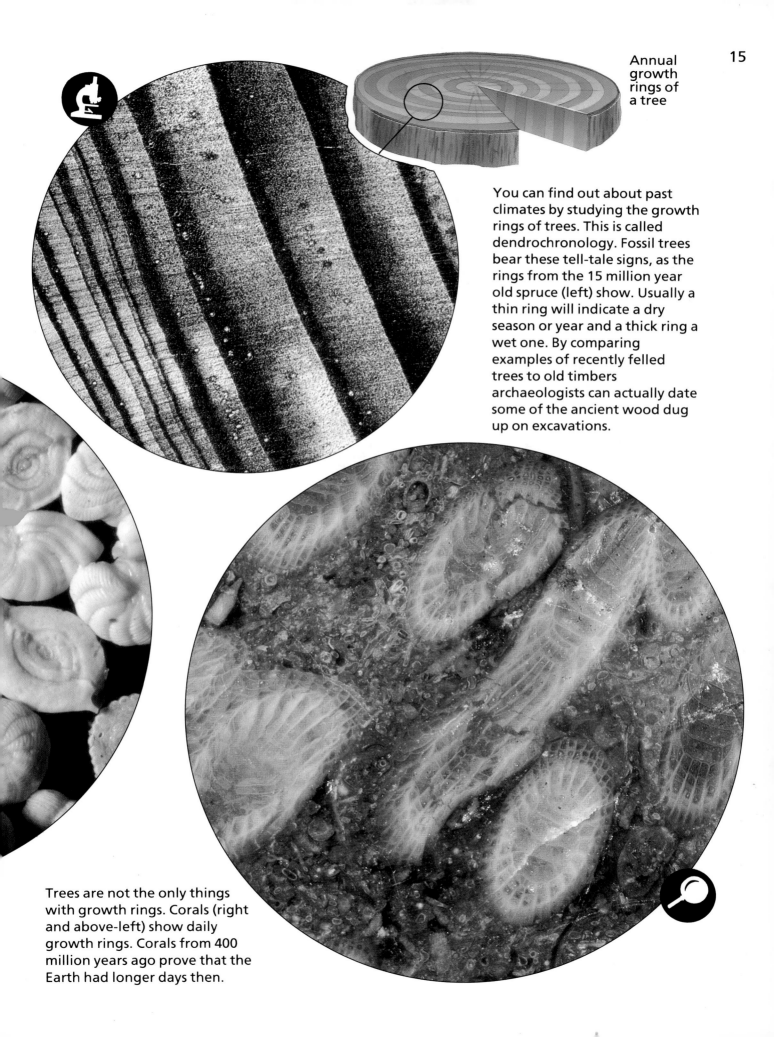

Annual growth rings of a tree

You can find out about past climates by studying the growth rings of trees. This is called dendrochronology. Fossil trees bear these tell-tale signs, as the rings from the 15 million year old spruce (left) show. Usually a thin ring will indicate a dry season or year and a thick ring a wet one. By comparing examples of recently felled trees to old timbers archaeologists can actually date some of the ancient wood dug up on excavations.

Trees are not the only things with growth rings. Corals (right and above-left) show daily growth rings. Corals from 400 million years ago prove that the Earth had longer days then.

EARLY PREHISTORIC PEOPLES

There have been human beings on Earth for at least 3 million years. Archaeologists have found fossil bones and the tools which people used. The most difficult job was to work out the dates for the bones they found and the order in which we developed from these earliest peoples. On the right are the fossil bones of the jaw and teeth of one of our early relatives called Australopithecus afarensis found in Ethiopia in Africa. Our human species (called Homo sapiens) probably spread out from Africa to Europe, Asia and Australia. We now know that people reached Australia about 40,000 years ago. We call all these early people hunter-gatherers because they had to exist by hunting, gathering and fishing for their food.

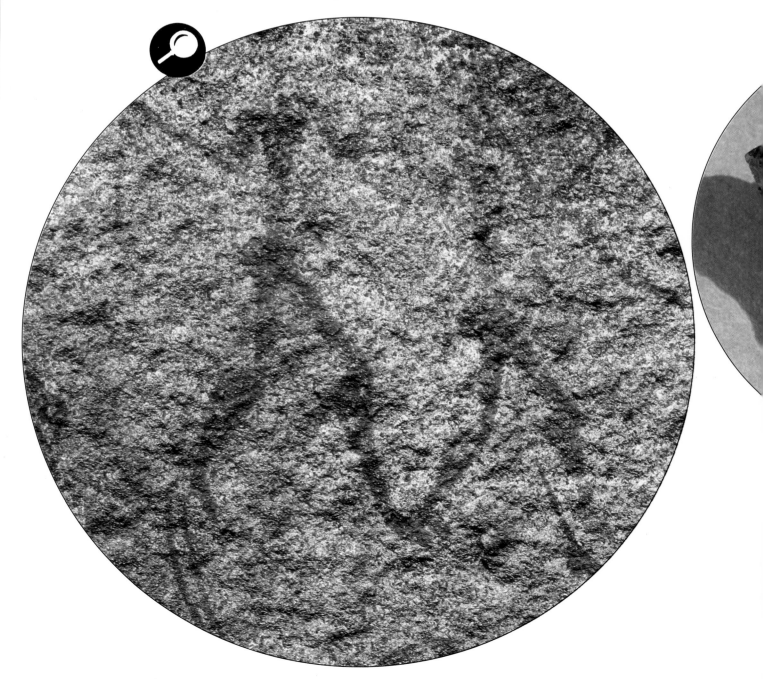

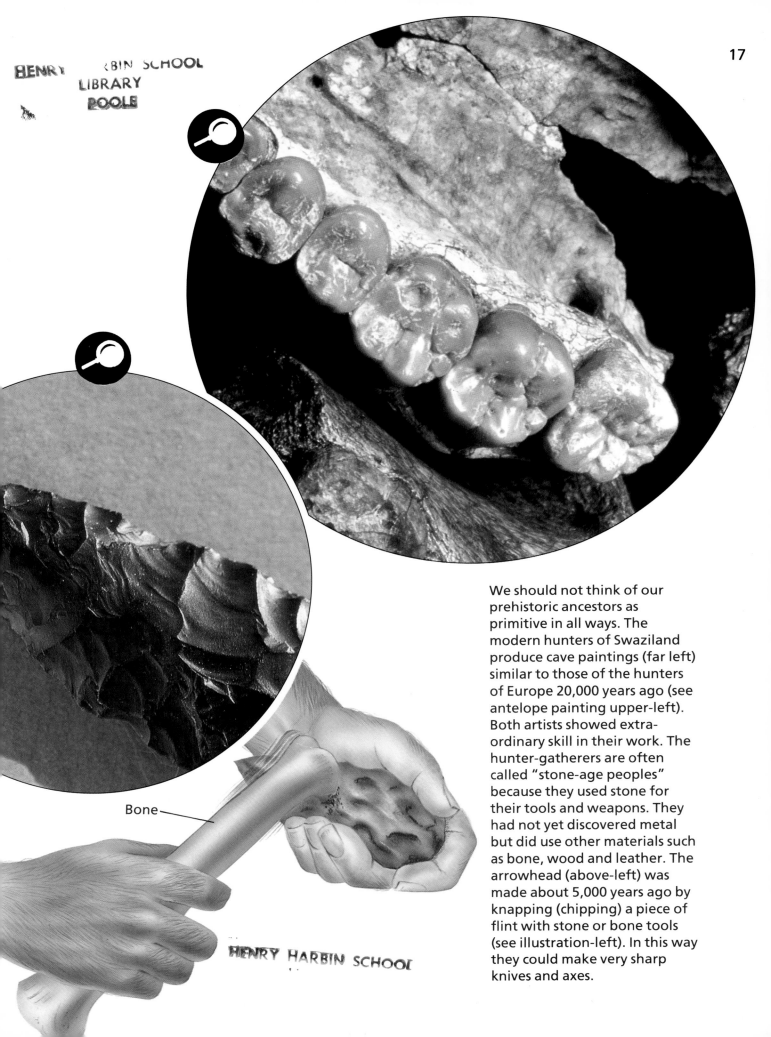

17

Bone

We should not think of our prehistoric ancestors as primitive in all ways. The modern hunters of Swaziland produce cave paintings (far left) similar to those of the hunters of Europe 20,000 years ago (see antelope painting upper-left). Both artists showed extraordinary skill in their work. The hunter-gatherers are often called "stone-age peoples" because they used stone for their tools and weapons. They had not yet discovered metal but did use other materials such as bone, wood and leather. The arrowhead (above-left) was made about 5,000 years ago by knapping (chipping) a piece of flint with stone or bone tools (see illustration-left). In this way they could make very sharp knives and axes.

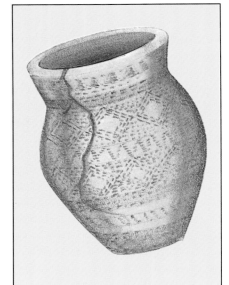

STUDYING POTTERY

Pottery is the word we use for any object made of clay which has been fired (baked) in a kiln or in a bonfire. Pottery was invented over 10,000 years ago and is the commonest artefact discovered by archaeologists on their excavations. Because the clay has been hardened by firing it is very difficult to destroy, although archaeologists usually find only broken pieces. Sometimes they are lucky enough to find whole pots, like the one below-left which was made about 4,000 years ago and buried with a dead person. Studying pottery helps us find out many things about the makers. For example, where they got their clay from, what sort of decoration they liked, what they used the pots for and how far afield they travelled or traded.

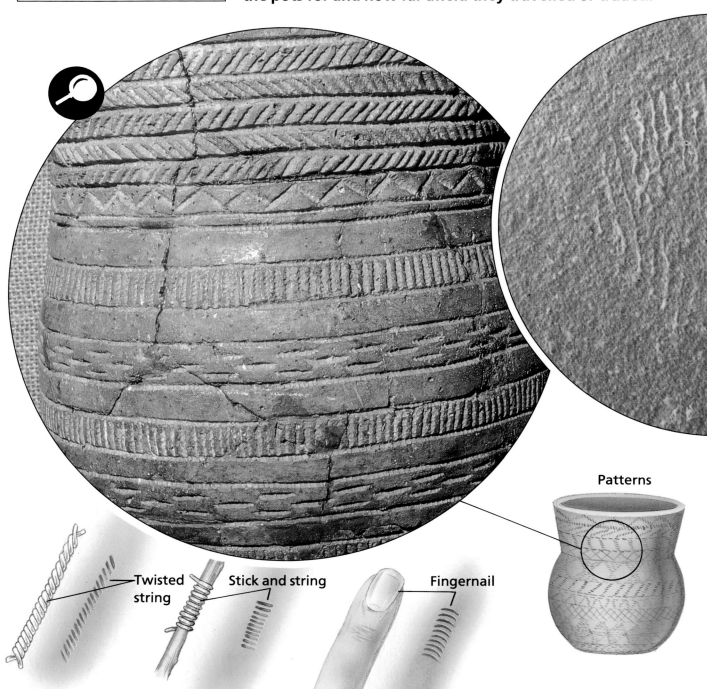

Twisted string

Stick and string

Fingernail

Patterns

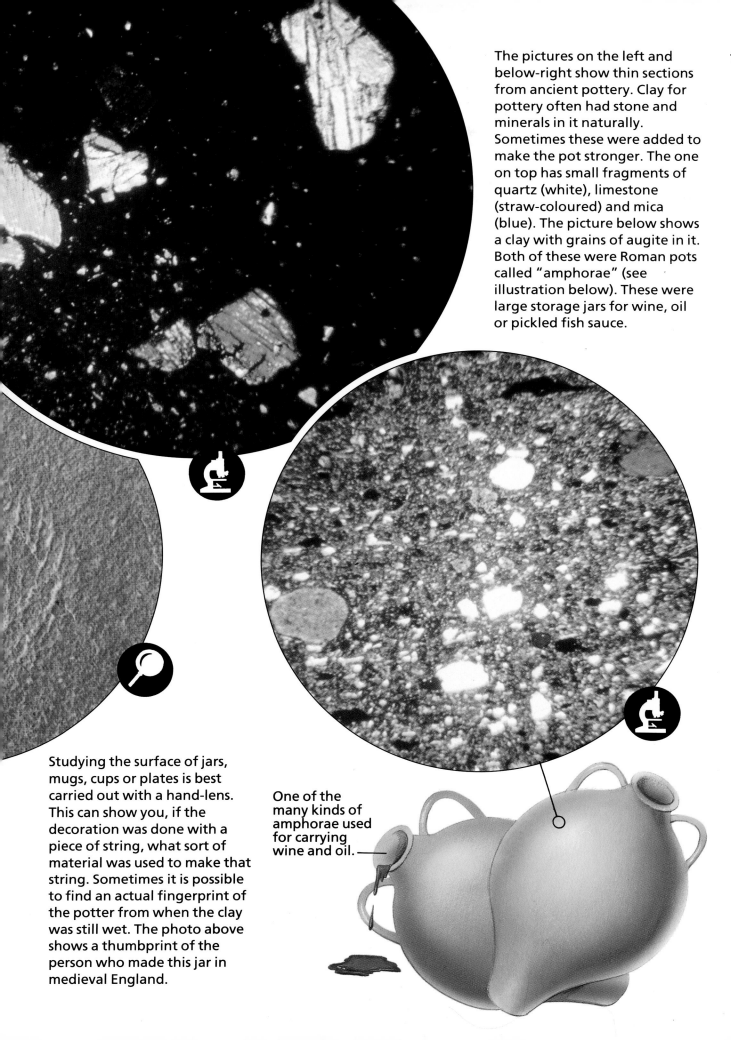

The pictures on the left and below-right show thin sections from ancient pottery. Clay for pottery often had stone and minerals in it naturally. Sometimes these were added to make the pot stronger. The one on top has small fragments of quartz (white), limestone (straw-coloured) and mica (blue). The picture below shows a clay with grains of augite in it. Both of these were Roman pots called "amphorae" (see illustration below). These were large storage jars for wine, oil or pickled fish sauce.

Studying the surface of jars, mugs, cups or plates is best carried out with a hand-lens. This can show you, if the decoration was done with a piece of string, what sort of material was used to make that string. Sometimes it is possible to find an actual fingerprint of the potter from when the clay was still wet. The photo above shows a thumbprint of the person who made this jar in medieval England.

One of the many kinds of amphorae used for carrying wine and oil.

BELIEFS AND RITUALS

The farmers of prehistory often worked together to build huge monuments of stone and earth. Some were great long or round burial mounds which have survived to this day and show they had beliefs about a life after death. Inside the burial mounds were chambers in which the bones of the dead were laid out. Sometimes pots (like the one on page 18) were buried with the dead. Some monuments, especially standing stones (left) or circles like Stonehenge, showed that special rituals or ceremonies were involved in their religious worship. Building these monuments needed great effort on the part of the prehistoric peoples since there were no machines to help cut and lift the stones or to move vast quantities of earth.

The seeds below were found during the excavation of a huge mound called Silbury Hill in Wiltshire, England, built around 4,500 years ago. It has been estimated that it was over 50 metres high originally and would have taken ten years to build if 500 people had worked on it every day! The seeds, grasses, beetles and flying ants preserved under the mound showed that the work must have been started in summer. So we know when and how it was built – but not why.

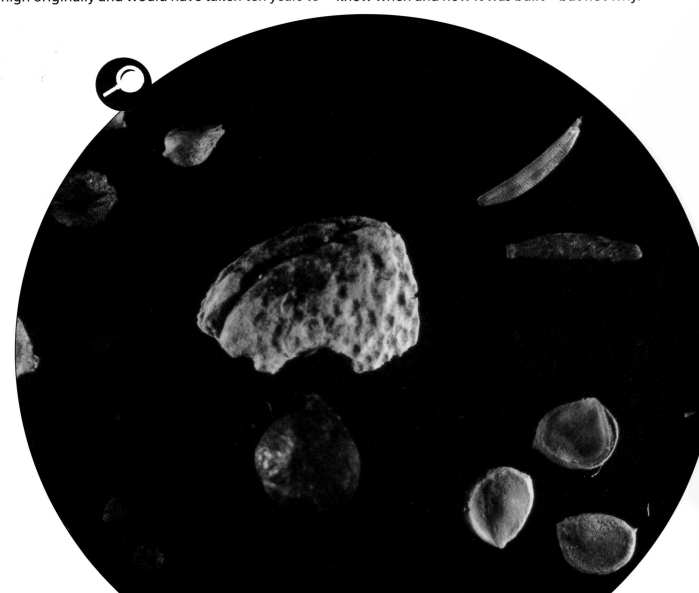

The Celts were people living in western Europe from about 700 BC. They were famous for their beautiful metalwork. The picture on the right here is from a bucket decorated with helmeted heads, animals and designs. The Celts believed that gods and spirits were everywhere and needed offerings and sacrifices made to them. Below is the head of "Tollund Man", who was probably a sacrificial victim. He was either hanged or strangled and then thrown into a peat bog in Denmark. His body was so well preserved that archaeologists have been able to identify his last meal from various seeds found in his stomach.

MUMMIES

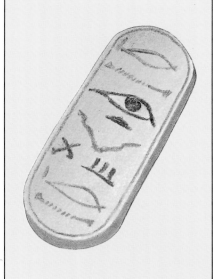

The ancient Egyptians believed there was a life after death. They thought that the dead went on a journey to the underworld where they would continue their lives as before. Kings would continue to be kings, rich merchants would enjoy their usual luxuries, servants would still fetch and carry, and so on. We know all this because archaeologists have unravelled the meaning of their hieroglyphs, or writing, like that seen on the left. The Egyptians thought it important that the body itself, as well as the person's possessions, should reach the underworld in good condition. A complicated process of mummification, to dry out the body, was developed to preserve the bodies of their dead.

Making a mummy involved first removing the internal organs which were placed in special jars. The body was dehydrated (dried out) using natron, a form of salt, to stop the flesh rotting. It was then wrapped in cloth and bandages (see right).

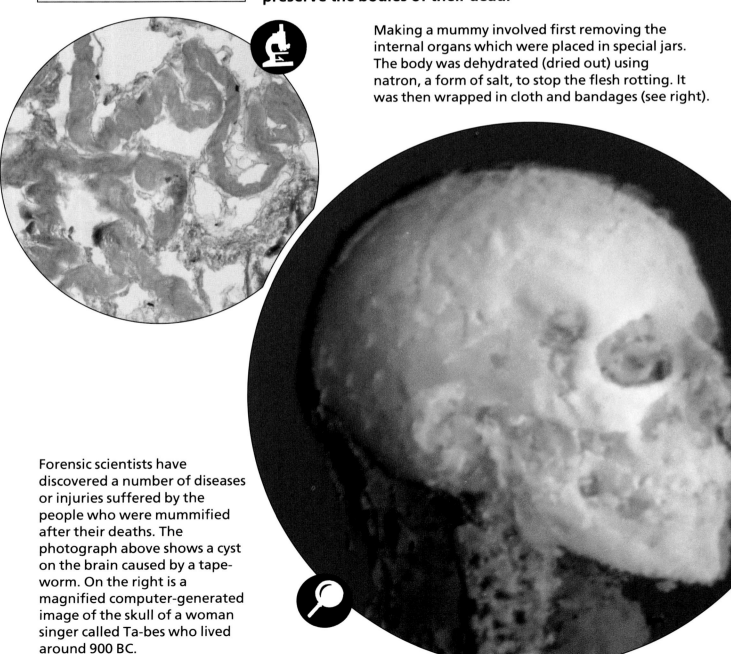

Forensic scientists have discovered a number of diseases or injuries suffered by the people who were mummified after their deaths. The photograph above shows a cyst on the brain caused by a tape-worm. On the right is a magnified computer-generated image of the skull of a woman singer called Ta-bes who lived around 900 BC.

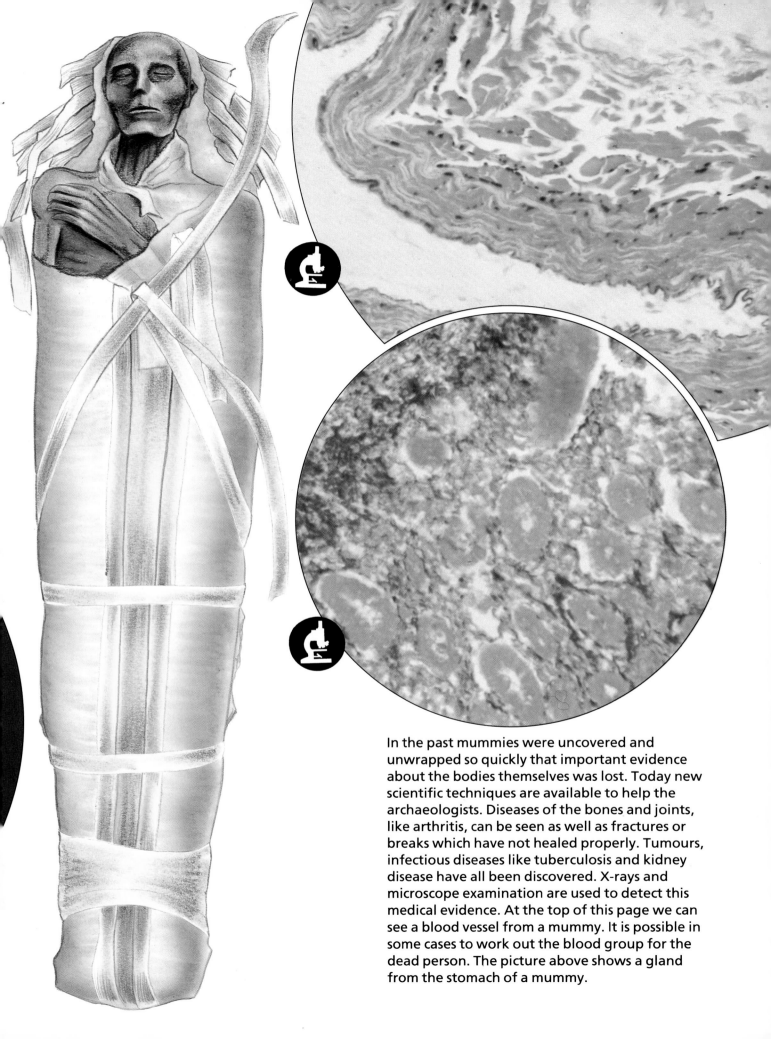

In the past mummies were uncovered and unwrapped so quickly that important evidence about the bodies themselves was lost. Today new scientific techniques are available to help the archaeologists. Diseases of the bones and joints, like arthritis, can be seen as well as fractures or breaks which have not healed properly. Tumours, infectious diseases like tuberculosis and kidney disease have all been discovered. X-rays and microscope examination are used to detect this medical evidence. At the top of this page we can see a blood vessel from a mummy. It is possible in some cases to work out the blood group for the dead person. The picture above shows a gland from the stomach of a mummy.

TELL-TALE FRAGMENTS

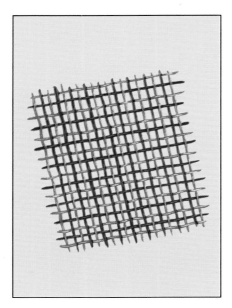

Archaeologists look for clues to help them understand what happened in the past. Some study fragments of objects, such as the sample of cloth illustrated on the left, to find out how things were made and what materials were used. At the same time, those who work in laboratories need to find ways of conserving the objects for people to study in the future, or to put on display in museums. These archaeologists are called conservators. They take X-ray photographs of objects before an examination takes place. The careful work of cleaning can be carried out using a low-powered binocular microscope. An electron microscope helps to identify the actual materials used originally, and what they have become.

Burial places often provide archaeologists with objects which can give us a picture of what people were wearing. The photograph above is of a circular brooch excavated in an Anglo-Saxon cemetery at West Heslerton in North Yorkshire, England. The cemetery was part of a very large village occupied between about AD 450 and AD 650. Archaeologists have found a number of objects buried with the dead – spears, knives and jewellery, and personal items such as brooches and buckles. This brooch, made of bronze, has an iron pin on the back to attach it to the person's clothes. A fragment of cloth has been preserved by iron corrosion. The photograph on the right shows that the cloth is woven wool and is perhaps the remains of a cloak or tunic.

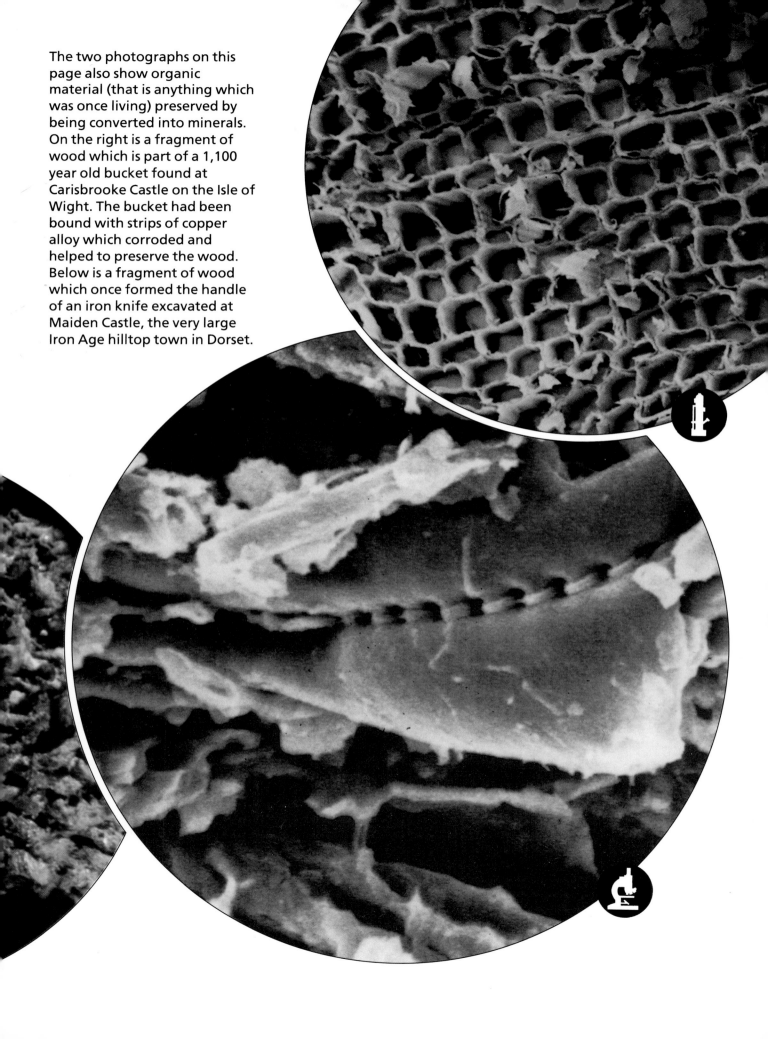

The two photographs on this page also show organic material (that is anything which was once living) preserved by being converted into minerals. On the right is a fragment of wood which is part of a 1,100 year old bucket found at Carisbrooke Castle on the Isle of Wight. The bucket had been bound with strips of copper alloy which corroded and helped to preserve the wood. Below is a fragment of wood which once formed the handle of an iron knife excavated at Maiden Castle, the very large Iron Age hilltop town in Dorset.

THE PAST IN THE PRESENT

Most archaeologists would say that studying the past helps us to understand more about the present. Archaeologists and palaeontologists use a range of scientific techniques to help them uncover fresh evidence and understand what went on. This book contains many micro-pictures taken with equipment developed for other purposes. However, a number of these techniques are used by scientists concerned with what happened recently rather than what happened millions of years ago. Geologists study ancient rocks to learn about the movements of the Earth's crust. Other scientists use such information to help find out when and where earthquakes and volcanoes are likely to threaten lives.

Petroleum oil, above-left, is our most valuable fossil fuel. When refined it is used to make gasoline, plastics, and chemicals.

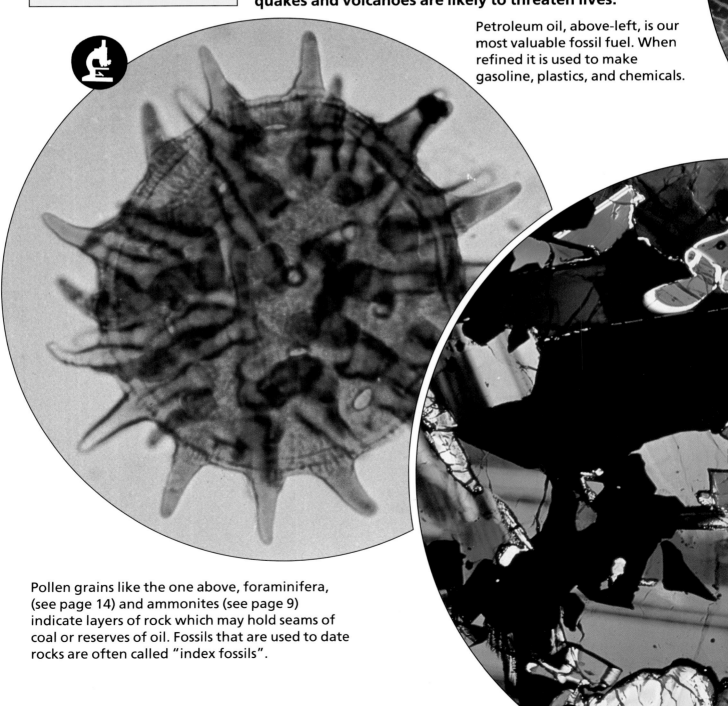

Pollen grains like the one above, foraminifera, (see page 14) and ammonites (see page 9) indicate layers of rock which may hold seams of coal or reserves of oil. Fossils that are used to date rocks are often called "index fossils".

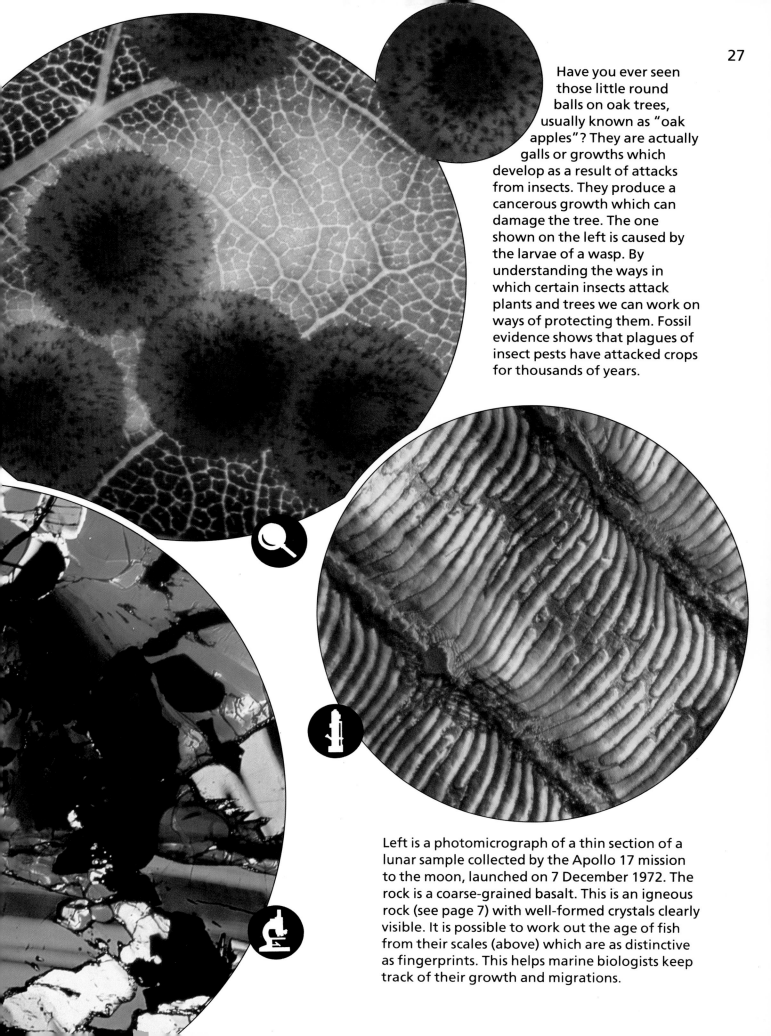

Have you ever seen those little round balls on oak trees, usually known as "oak apples"? They are actually galls or growths which develop as a result of attacks from insects. They produce a cancerous growth which can damage the tree. The one shown on the left is caused by the larvae of a wasp. By understanding the ways in which certain insects attack plants and trees we can work on ways of protecting them. Fossil evidence shows that plagues of insect pests have attacked crops for thousands of years.

Left is a photomicrograph of a thin section of a lunar sample collected by the Apollo 17 mission to the moon, launched on 7 December 1972. The rock is a coarse-grained basalt. This is an igneous rock (see page 7) with well-formed crystals clearly visible. It is possible to work out the age of fish from their scales (above) which are as distinctive as fingerprints. This helps marine biologists keep track of their growth and migrations.

PRACTICAL PROJECTS

You can discover a great deal about nature's miniature world with just a hand-lens. But to see greater detail you will need a standard, or "home", microscope. Anything you want to study must be mounted on a glass slide. They should be delicate items or things which are cut so thinly that you can see through them. To make slides you may need special dyes to stain your specimen so that your eye can pick out different cells. The way to do this is outlined below. If you are going to try something tricky, it is worth asking for help from an experienced adult, perhaps at school. Some microscope suppliers will sell ready-made slides. These are often of excellent quality and not expensive. If you do start to make your own slides, or buy ones that you like, be careful to store them properly.

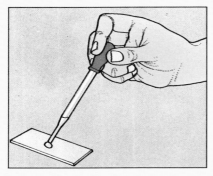

To prepare a cell slide, place a drop of clean water containing the cells on the glass.

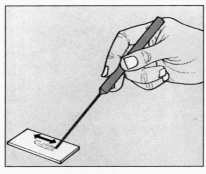

With a wire loop that has been sterilized in a flame, spread the fluid thinly and let it dry.

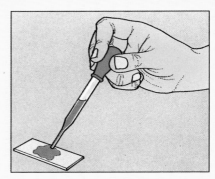

Add a small drop of staining dye to the cells and leave for a few minutes.

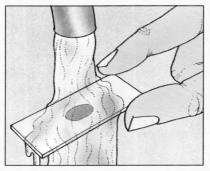

Wash off the dye with water or alcohol. You can stain with another, contrasting dye.

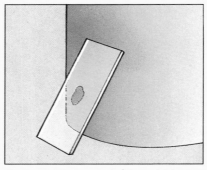

Leave the slide to dry. You can speed up drying by gently warming the slide over a flame.

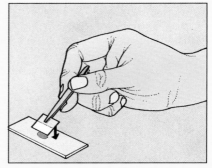

Place a cover slip (a thin square of glass) over the stained cells, using a pair of tweezers.

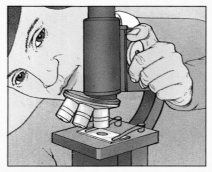

Put the slide on the microscope stage and position the mirror to give you good illumination.

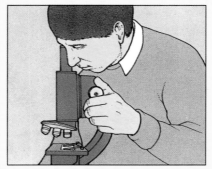

Select the objective lens you want, then move the eyepiece up and down to focus. Start at the lowest magnification.

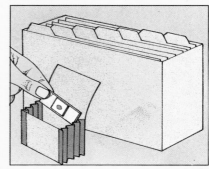

Keep your prepared slides in a wallet made from a folded sheet of thin card, which will protect them from dust.

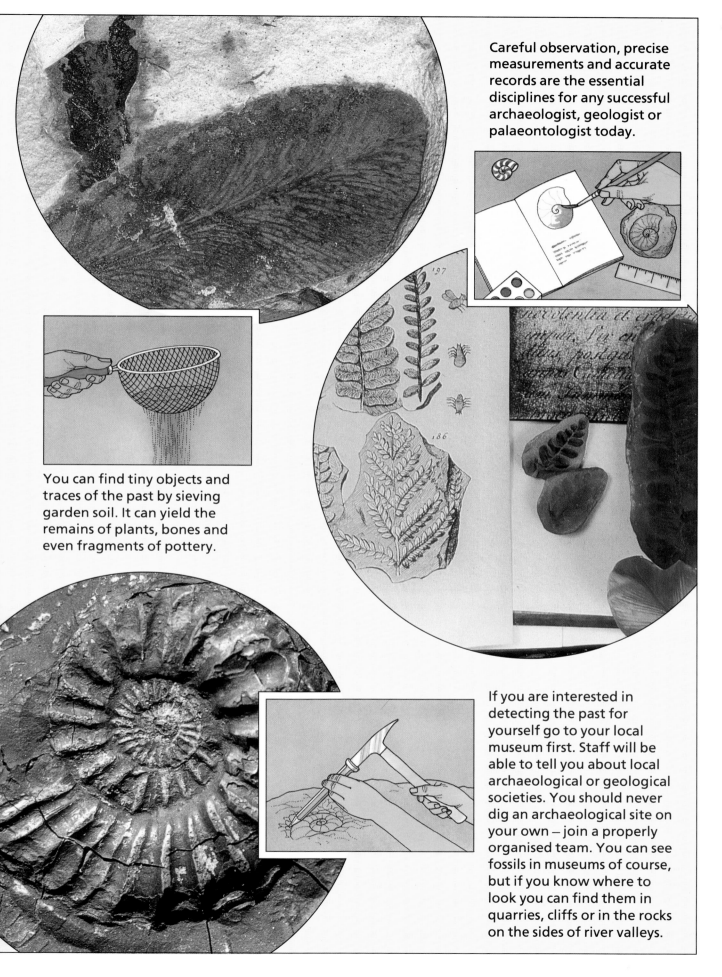

Careful observation, precise measurements and accurate records are the essential disciplines for any successful archaeologist, geologist or palaeontologist today.

You can find tiny objects and traces of the past by sieving garden soil. It can yield the remains of plants, bones and even fragments of pottery.

If you are interested in detecting the past for yourself go to your local museum first. Staff will be able to tell you about local archaeological or geological societies. You should never dig an archaeological site on your own – join a properly organised team. You can see fossils in museums of course, but if you know where to look you can find them in quarries, cliffs or in the rocks on the sides of river valleys.

MICROPHOTOGRAPHY

Some of the photographs in this book were taken using a camera with special close-up lenses that magnify the subject in much the same way as a hand-lens would magnify them for your eye. Others, with greater magnification, were taken by fitting a camera to the eyepiece of a scientific microscope. Such photos are known as photomicrographs. The colours in these are often those of stains used, rather than natural colours. If you have a home microscope you can take your own photomicrographs. You will need a single lens reflex camera and a special camera attachment. However, these pictures will not be able to match the magnification produced when using a scanning electron microscope.

You can make a collection of fossils yourself. Take careful notes when "in the field" and make sure you label your specimens properly. After all you are the curator of your own museum! Give each specimen a number, write the date you found it, the type of rock it came from, and its exact location. The illustrations below show how to make fossil casts.

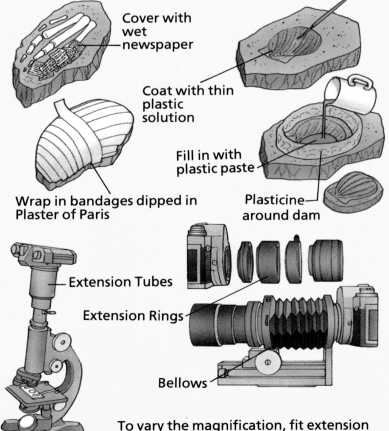

Cover with wet newspaper

Coat with thin plastic solution

Fill in with plastic paste

Wrap in bandages dipped in Plaster of Paris

Plasticine around dam

Extension Tubes

Extension Rings

Bellows

To vary the magnification, fit extension rings or bellows to the camera attachment.

There are two main types of electron microscope. In a transmission type (TEM), a beam of electrons is passed through an extremely thin slice of tissue and an image is produced on a screen. In a scanning electron microscope (SEM), a fine beam of electrons is moved across the surface of the tissue for reflections to be collected and used to create an image on a television type of screen. Using an SEM, realistic 3-D images are produced. But as with all types of microscope specimens, the tissues and organs are no longer alive. The slide preparation process kills live cells. The colours on photos produced using an SEM are false colours added in processing.

GLOSSARY

AD is an abbreviation for Anno Domini which means "in the year of our Lord" and is used for all dates after the birth of Christ. For example, this book was published in AD 1990.

amphorae were very large two-handled containers used by the ancient Greeks and Romans to transport wine, olive oil and pickled fish sauce.

artefact a man-made or artificial product.

BC stands for "before Christ" and is used for all dates up to Christ's birth.

crust is the word used for the outer layer around the earth on which we live. The crust is made up from three types of rock – igneous, sedimentary and metamorphic.

dendrochronology is the system for dating wood from ancient sites by counting the annual growth rings.

dinosaurs were prehistoric reptiles which became extinct about 65 million years ago.

fossils are the preserved remains of animals and plants.

glacial is a period of time when conditions were colder and ice-sheets (glaciers) covered the landscape. Warmer periods in between are called interglacials. Some people call glacial periods "Ice Ages".

ichthyosaurs were prehistoric swimming reptiles.

igneous rocks form part of the earth's crust and were once molten material, such as lava from a volcanic eruption.

Iron Age is the name archaeologists give to the period in Europe when people used iron for their tools and weapons. In Britain the Iron Age lasted from about 700 BC to AD 43.

magma is the molten rock below the earth's crust.

metamorphic rocks are sedimentary or igneous rocks which have been changed by pressure, heat or chemical action.

mineral-preservation can occur in organic material when it comes into contact with metal corrosion.

mummies are the dried and preserved remains of bodies of people and animals.

organic materials are anything which was once living, such as wood or bone.

petrification is the changing to stone of organic material. Fossils are often petrified animals, trees or plants.

plesiosaurs were prehistoric swimming reptiles.

pollen is a powdery substance found in flowering plants and trees. Its transfer between different parts of plants is what makes new flowers grow.

pterosaurs were prehistoric flying reptiles.

sedimentary rocks are the remains of sediments like mud and sand from long-vanished oceans and seas.

X-ray photographs enable scientists to study the details of objects invisible to the naked eye.

WEIGHTS AND MEASURES

mm = millimetres 10mm = 4/10 inch
cm = centimetre 100cm = 1m = 3 feet
m = metre 1000m = 1km = 6/10 mile
km = kilometre
lb = pound

g = gram 1000g = 1kg = 2lb 3oz
kg = kilogram
0.1 = 1/10
0.01 = 1/100
0.001 = 1/1000

INDEX

Photographic Credits:
Cover: Topham Picture Library; title page and pages 9 top, 10 left, 11 right, 14 right and 15 top: Ardea; pages 6 left, 7 bottom, 11 left and 29 top: Geo-science Features; pages 6 right, 8 and 17 left: Bruce Coleman Ltd; pages 7 top, 10 right, 12 both, 13 both, 16, 17 right, 22 right, 26 right, 27 both and 29 middle and bottom: Science Photo Library; pages 8-9, 14 left and 15 bottom: Biophoto Associates; page 9 bottom: British Museum/Natural History/Oxford Scientific Films; page 18 left: Photosources; pages 18 right, 24 and 25: English Heritage; page 19 both: Dr David Williams; page 20: Alexander Keiller Museum; page 21 top: Silkeborg Museum, Denmark; page 21 bottom: Ronald Sheridan; pages 22 left and 23 both: Dept of Histopathology, Royal Preston Hospital; page 26 left: Shell.

PRINTED IN BELGIUM BY
proost
INTERNATIONAL BOOK PRODUCTION